G000310709

FAMILY WALKS
in
BERKSHIRE
and
NORTH HAMPSHIRE

Kathy Sharp

Scarthin Books, Cromford, Derbyshire 1991

FAMILY WALKS
IN BERKSHIRE AND NORTH HAMPSHIRE

Family Walks Series
General Editor: Norman Taylor

THE COUNTRY CODE

Enjoy the countryside and respect its life and work
Guard against all risk of fire
Fasten all gates
Keep your dogs under close control
Keep to public paths across farmland
Use gates and stiles to cross fences, hedges and walls
Leave livestock, crops and machinery alone
Take your litter home
Help to keep all water clean
Protect wildlife, plants and trees
Take special care on country roads
Make no unnecessary noise

Published 1991

Phototypesetting, printing by Higham Press Ltd., Shirland, Derbyshire

© Kathy Sharp 1991

No part of this book may be reproduced in any form or by any means without the permission of the Owner of the Copyright.

ISBN 0 907758 37 1

RIVER ALRE AT ALRESFORD   Route 12

1

PREFACE

My parents introduced me to the habit of going out into the countryside at weekends, and it is a tradition I passed on to my daughter Nina as soon as she was old enough to walk. Family walking is a painless and natural way for children to develop a sense of the past in the setting of the changing seasons - an invaluable gift to any child in this high-tech world. It also happens to be good fun.

I am sure that readers following in our footsteps in the Berkshire and North Hampshire area will find as much beauty, charm, curiosity, surprise and fun there as we did.

Happy walking!

Dedication

To Norman, Bette and Christine Fox. Remembering linnets by the old railway.

Acknowledgements and Thanks

To Norman Champ for good advice, and especially to Roy Sharp for taking the photographs and for all the help.

About the Author

Kathy Sharp was born in Kent, but has lived on the fringes of the Berkshire and North Hampshire area for the past nineteen years. Together with her husband and daughter, she has explored much of this attractive countryside over the years. She works at the Adult Education Institute in Spelthorne, Surrey, teaching natural history and leading country walks for students, as well as acting as Publicity Officer for the Institute.

CONTENTS

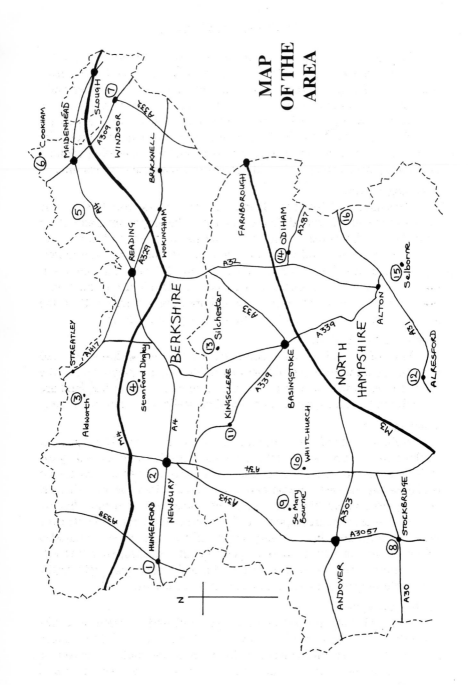

MAP
OF THE
AREA

4

INTRODUCTION

This book is designed to help families with children explore the countryside of Berkshire and North Hampshire, and to get the most from their walks. The routes range from one and three quarter to seven and a half miles in length, allowing for all ages, and cover a variety of landscapes. Where possible, the walks are arranged with a pub for refreshments around the half way point. The "attractions" section for each walk is a selection of local points of interest, including wildlife, landscape, local history and buildings, chosen to amuse all the family.

Choosing a Walk

Berkshire and Northern Hampshire is a gentle countryside, and none of the walks is very difficult. The list in the Appendix grades them according to the slopes of the hills, from flat to steep, and in order of length. Very young children should begin with the shorter, flatter routes, or you can choose just part of the route. Routes 1, 3 and 13 are figure-of-eight, and the loops can be used independently. Don't be too ambitious - no-one will enjoy themselves if the children are exhausted. Save the longer walks until they are older and will enjoy the challenge.

How Long Will It Take?

Most of the walks are intended as a day's outing, with time allowed for looking at interesting buildings or wildlife, and for play. Some of the shorter ones, however, can be completed in half a day or less, and are specially suitable for spring or autumn when daylight hours are restricted.

What To Wear

Walking is good exercise, and you soon get warm. Thin layers of clothing that can be peeled off are the most comfortable, especially for children. Waterproofs are essential - the lightweight variety that can be packed away are best. Please make sure the children stay dry -there is nothing more miserable than completing a long walk in damp, clammy clothes. Shoes, too. are important. The routes in this book do not cover very rough ground, but ordinary shoes will leave your feet and ankles aching. Invest in hiking boots or good quality trainers; your feet will thank you forever. Finally, don't forget a really capacious, lightweight bag, preferably waterproof, for all your bits and pieces.

Finding the Way

Although they are not essential, you will find it helpful to equip yourself with copies of the local Ordnance Survey maps: map references are given for each route. Most of the footpaths on the routes are clear and well-marked, but where they are at all obscure I have taken extra care in describing them and any landmarks nearby. One or two may occasionally be disturbed by farming activities, especially ploughing. In this case take the shortest detour round the field edge and rejoin the path as soon as possible.

Refreshments

All the pubs and inns marked on the routes have gardens, and many have impressive play areas guaranteed to delight children. Some have children's rooms, and most allow children inside provided you are buying food, and provided they are well behaved. Extended opening hours now mean that pubs can stay open until 3 p.m., but bear in mind, if you want lunch, that catering usually stops around 2 p.m. Remember, too, that not all landlords choose to stay open until 3 p.m. (they're not obliged to), especially in winter. Lastly, don't bring your packed lunches into pub gardens to eat - landlords tend to take a dim view of this, even if you are buying drinks.

Public Transport

Many of the walks can be reached by bus or train - a very green example to set the children! It may be necessary to begin the walk at a slightly different point on the route, but this shouldn't cause any problems. Be aware, though, that not all bus routes operate on Sundays. Brief details of bus operators are given with each route where available, and numbers to ring for timetables are included in the Appendix.

KENNET AND AVON CANAL

Symbols used on the route maps

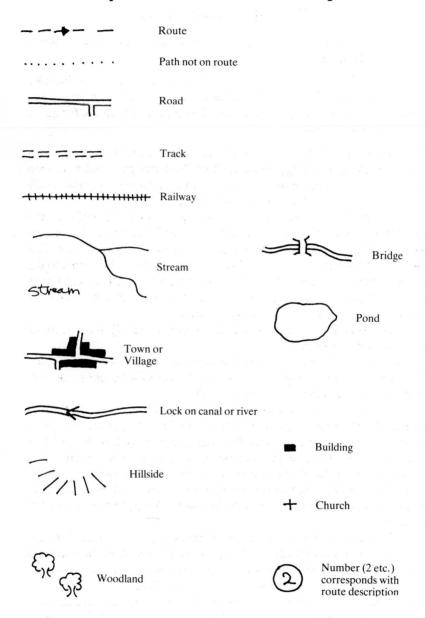

Route

Path not on route

Road

Track

Railway

Stream

Stream

Bridge

Pond

Town or Village

Lock on canal or river

Building

Hillside

Church

Woodland

Number (2 etc.) corresponds with route description

Kennet & Avon Canal

Outline Hungerford ~ Kennet & Avon Canal ~ Froxfield ~ North Standen ~ Hungerford.

Summary Canal towpaths make good walks, and this route includes substantial stretches of the Kennet and Avon Canal, seen from both banks. It is rich in wildlife and lies in a beautiful valley on the fringes of Berkshire and Wiltshire.

Attractions Hungerford is a small country town with a history as a coaching stop and staging post on the Bath Road that goes back to Roman times. It is better known these days as an antique-fancier's paradise, with well over 20 antique shops in the High Street.

But there is another highway running through Hungerford - the Kennet and Avon Canal. This great waterway links Bristol in the west with the Thames at Reading in the East and is nearly 90 miles long. This meant that the water traffic could travel from the Bristol Channel to the Thames estuary - quite a feat. It was completed in sections and finally opened in 1810. Like many of our canals it later fell into sad disrepair, unable to face competition from the railways.

However, like the Basingstoke Canal (see route 14), it has recently been reopened to craft.

The towpaths are in good repair now, and provide excellent walks. The locks are in working order, some with neat lock-keeper's cottages, some of them out in the fields, unattended.

Picketfield Lock still seems almost derelict, with grasses, thistles and pink herb robert growing abundantly on the shady side of the lock gate - on the gate itself, that is, and that pale green waxy fern is the black spleenwort, sprouting happily on the walls. And there is lush growth of campion and willowherb overhanging the rushing outflow on the downstream side. It seems remote and untouched, with only its name, neatly printed on the upstream gate like all the locks, to remind us of its purpose.

There are the remains of several former bridges to be seen along the canal, if you look carefully - little chunks of brickwork in the bank and rusty diamond shaped roadsigns half-hidden in the undergrowth. Children might enjoy seeing how many they can find.

In the low wet fields within sight of the large spire of Hungerford church, the walk passes through Hungerford Marsh. It is a nature

continued on page 12

Route 1

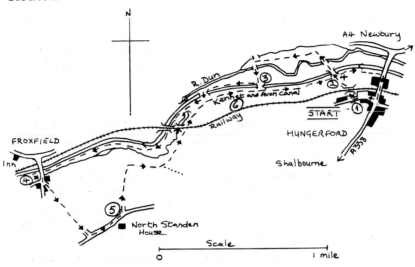

CANAL AT HUNGERFORD

10

Route 1

Kennet & Avon Canal 4½ miles

START   *Hungerford town centre, 8 miles west of Newbury on the A4. Park at the car park in Church Street (O.S. Sheet 174 SU337685).*

ROUTE

1. *From the car park turn right and follow Church Street to the junction with Croft Road. Turn right and go under the railway bridge. Turn left around the green and then right into the churchyard. Follow the path past the church and come out on to the canal bank.*
2. *Cross the swing bridge over the canal, and the stile beyond. Follow the path into Hungerford Marsh. Cross the next bridge, over the River Dun, and follow the track round to the left. Cross the river again by the small weir and continue along the path. At the two bridges, cross the one on the left and go across the pasture to Marsh Lock.*
3. *Turn right without crossing the canal, and follow the bank to the next lock (Cobblers Lock). Go through the small white gate and cross the canal by the lock bridge. Turn right and follow the tow path. Cross a stile, and continue, going under a railway bridge and passing Picketfield Lock.*
4. *On reaching the road bridge, go underneath and then up on to the road at Froxfield. If you wish to stop for refreshment here, cross the bridge and follow the road, turning left at the next junction - the Watermeadow Inn is nearby. If not, turn right and follow the road to the next junction, taking the bridle path marked "North Standen" on the left beyond the first house. Follow the path uphill. On meeting the road, turn left (look out for the Berkshire/Wiltshire county boundary marker in the hedge).*
5. *Pass North Standen House, then take the marked footpath on the left. At the gate at the far end, turn right and follow the trackway. Go through the gap at the field end and continue until the track turns right. Turn left and follow the field edge downhill. At the bottom cross the stile and go across the railway (take care). Cross the stile on the far side and walk across the pasture towards the lock house. (Look out for the three arched aqueduct that carries the canal across the river.) Cross the stile on to the canal bank and turn right.*
6. *Follow the tow path past Marsh Lock, back past the church, all the way to Hungerford Bridge. Turn right at the bridge and follow the high street to the junction with Church Street. Turn right and walk back to the starting point.*

ALTERNATIVE ROUTE
It is possible to make a far shorter walk by following the route as in numbers 1 and 2 above, crossing the canal at Marsh Lock, and then completing the walk as in 6.

ACCESS BY BUS
There are bus services to Swindon and Newbury and rail services to London.

---

reserve, a lovely wet area, covered in yellow irises and reed beds, with the little River Dun flowing quietly through, with the sedge warblers buzzing and chattering in the reeds.

Refreshments   plenty of choice in Hungerford, or the halfway point of the walk is at Froxfield, where the Watermeadow Inn has a large garden and play area.

DONNINGTON CASTLE

12

Donnington Castle and Snelsmore Common

Outline   Bagnor village ~ Snelsmore Common ~ Donnington Castle ~ Bagnor.

Summary   Although Donnington is only just outside the town of Newbury, this walk over the gently hilly country nearby is very rural and undisturbed. The castle itself is included as a reminder of the turbulent past of this now quiet landscape where the valleys of the Lambourn and Kennet meet.

Attractions   Snelsmore Common is a wonderful sandy open space, with birch woodland, tracts of heather and damp boggy areas which contain some interesting and unusual plants. One of the commoner ones, though, is the tormentil, a small trailing relative of the rose, with elegant five-fingered leaves and bright yellow flowers. There are lovely foxgloves in the woods, too.

An uncommon bird to look for is the tree pipit, a typical heathland bird. It sings on the wing like a lark, but starts and finishes its songflight from a treetop, not the ground. Look out, too for adders. This is just their kind of country and they turn up most often among bracken. The collapsed brown fronds of this tall fern exactly match the zig-zag pattern on the snakes' backs, and makes them very hard to see. This is as good a reason as any for keeping to the pathways, where any snake would be much more conspicuous.

Nearby, Donnington Castle, although mostly ruined, remains an impressive landmark. It was a tough stronghold in its day, guarding the crossing of the great west road and the Oxford road. Most of the damage to it was done in the days of the Civil War, when the Royalist garrison held out against a siege for twenty months - surrendering only when King Charles himself did. The magnificent gatehouse bears the scars - a large hole in one tower patched with red brick where it was hit by mortar fire. The towers are decorated with stone heads and gargoyles - children might enjoy trying to find any two the same - we couldn't. The outlines of a further four towers can be clearly traced in the stumps of the tall, medieval walls.

Donnington, on its little hill, has a wonderful commanding view along the valley of the Kennet, and to the high, bare downs beyond.

At Bagnor there is something unexpected - a tiny, exquisite nature reserve, Rack Marsh, bordering the river Lambourn which runs through the village. This is the clearest and cleanest of bubbling chalk streams,

continued on page 16

Route 2

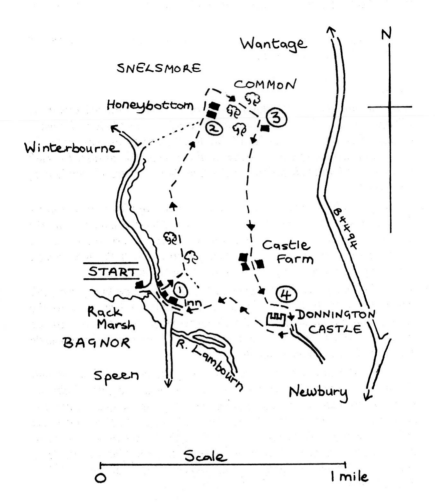

Route 2

Donnington Castle and Snelsmore Common   2¾ miles

START   *Bagnor village 1½ miles N.W. of Newbury. (O.S. Sheet 174 SU454693). Park in the village.*

ROUTE

1. *Begin at the Blackbird, Bagnor. Facing the inn, turn left along the village street, and turn right on to the trackway just before the white cottage. Pass the remains of a stile on the left, and go straight across the field on the trodden path, crossing another stile on the far side. Turn left into the woodland belt and follow the path. Ignore a second path joining from the left.*

2. *Keep left of Honeybottom Cottage and continue uphill on to Snelsmore Common. Continue ahead at the hilltop for a short distance, then take the path downhill on the right, following the powerlines. Cross the damp area at the hill bottom, then go up through the woodlands, following the powerlines, and pass a still pool on the right.*

3. *Just before the powerlines branch in two, turn right on to a gravel path and follow it to the marked footpath to Donnington Castle. Leave the common and follow the fenced path across the fields. The castle can be glimpsed through the trees in the distance. Continue through Castle Farm, and down to the castle itself.*

4. *After investigating the castle (and admiring the view), follow the path downhill, through the car park, and out through the gates. Take the marked footpath on the right immediately beyond the gates. Cross the stile at the end, and follow the trodden path across the field to the next stile. Cross it and continue downhill through the meadow. At the end cross the stile and turn left on to the marked footpath. Cross the field and come out through the gate. Follow the gravel lane ahead back into Bagnor village.*

trickling through an "unimproved" meadow full of water plants, butterflies, birds and dragonflies, and it is well worth taking a little time to follow the path through. But be warned - it can be very wet underfoot, even in a dry season.

Refreshments   The Blackbird at Bagnor has a garden and play area and serves food at weekends.

ALDWORTH CHURCH

Aldworth & the Ridge Way Path

Outline   Ridge Way Path ~ Streatley Warren ~ Aldworth ~ Westridge
Green ~ Ridge Way Path.

Summary   The Thames passes through a gap in the Berkshire downs at
Streatley, close to the Oxfordshire border. This walk explores the
downland nearby, passing through the open grassland of Thurle Down
and Streatley Warren, on the way to Aldworth, a tiny village with a big
history, set at the base of the downs.

Attractions   Aldworth is a tiny village - just a clutch of houses, an
old-fashioned inn, a little post office and a church, all arranged round a
leafy back road of high hedges and blind corners. But it is worth a closer
look. There is the village well, by the inn -sensibly closed off now as it is
more than 350 feet deep, one of the deepest in all England. And there is
the old school, with its decorative acorn on one corner. Aldworth was
once a self-contained little place at the foot of the downs. But its history
goes back much further; in Norman times this place belonged to the
powerful de la Beche family. They had a castle nearby, though now there
is no trace of it - just a farm bearing the name de la Beche.

But in Aldworth church - a perfectly ordinary country church - the de
la Beche family left some spectacular traces. There are nine stone effigies
representing members of the family, and they are known as the Aldworth
Giants. These statues seem to fill the whole church, despite damage
sustained in Cromwell's time - indeed one of them lost his head - but even
after 700 years, the impression is of a family that completely dominated
the area. The church certainly isn't big enough for them, and the
atmosphere is cool and rather creepy. The largest male effigy became
known in the village as John Long, and three of the others as John Strong,
John Never Afraid and John Ever Afraid. The latter had asked to be
buried neither in the church nor the churchyard, so they rather
enterprisingly buried him under the church wall. The arch where his
effigy stood remains by the door, but poor John Ever Afraid himself is
gone.

The church still has something older than the Aldworth Giants - a
battered and strangulated yew tree. It is 1000 or more years old now, and
has a deadly nightshade plant growing at the broken foot of its trunk - a
very poisonous pair.

The downland around the Ridgeway Path is bare and open, with
distant views opening up and closing as you walk. There is nothing to hear

continued on page 20

Route 3

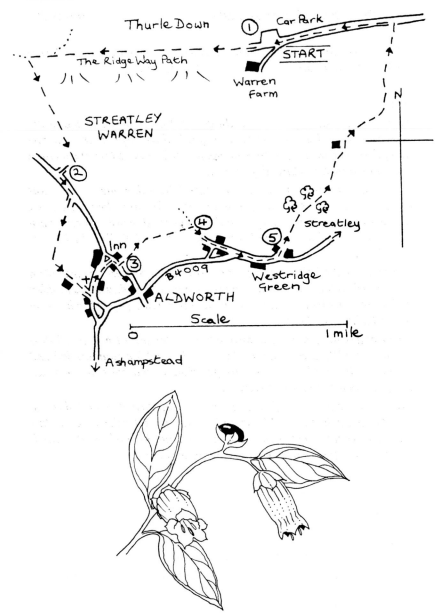

DEADLY NIGHTSHADE Atropa belladonna.   Greenish purple   June-Sept.
Shiny black beries.   POISONOUS.

18

Route 3

Aldworth & the Ridge Way Path   4½ miles

START   *The Ridge Way, one mile north west of Streatley. Park at the car park by Warren Farm (O.S. Sheet 174 SU567813).*

ROUTE

1. *From the car park follow the Ridgeway Path uphill and along the downtop, with Thurle Down on the right. Follow the path for about one mile, then take the major track on the left, following a line of telegraph poles downhill on to Streatley Warren.*

2. *At the junction with a paved road, turn left, follow the road a short distance, then turn right on to a stony track. This track later becomes a paved road. Continue along it until it reaches Aldworth church. Turn left at the road junction and follow the road uphill. The Bell Inn is straight ahead.*

3. *Turn right at the Bell and continue a short distance before turning left on to the marked footpath. This begins as a lane and continues as a trodden path across the fields. Follow it, passing through a gap in the hedge at the end of the first field.*

4. *At the end of the second field turn right on to the stony track, and follow it down into Westridge Green. At the main road junction turn left and continue downhill. Pass Westridge Manor and take the marked footpath on the left immediately after.*

5. *Follow the path through the farmyard and then downhill through woods and out into the fields beyond. At the old redbrick cottage, follow the track round to the right and continue until the track meets a road. Turn left and follow the road back to the car park.*

but the larks and the bleating of sheep - unless you are very lucky and hear a quail. Their soft calls of "whit-me-whit" or "wet-my-lips", repeated quickly, seem to come from all directions at once - quail are accomplished ventriloquists. But you could wait all day, or all week, and never set eyes on these secretive little game birds, invisible in the soft grasses.

The Ridge Way is a very ancient roadway - quite possibly the oldest in Britain. This rough stony track stretches across from west to east, and is now cared for as a long distance footpath.

Be aware that the Ridge Way Path is open to motor traffic, though apparently not used too frequently.

Refreshments The Bell Inn, Aldworth, has a garden and serves snacks at weekends.

STANFORD DINGLEY CHURCH

Stanford Dingley

Outline   Stanford Dingley ~ River Pang ~ Bushnells Green ~ Stanford Dingley.

Summary   A peaceful walk in fields and woodlands in the valley of the River Pang, full of birds, butterflies and wild flowers.

Attractions   Stanford Dingley, apart from its irresistible name, is a very pretty village with a remote air. Its houses are mostly old, with some lovely redbrick cottages and a couple of perfect Georgian houses. The residents have made some wonderful gardens, too.

There is a small church with a white weatherboarded tower, dedicated to the French Saint Denys - a rare choice - and there is an unusual gravestone just by the gate. It bears a sundial with a Latin inscription which says, loosely translated "Used well, or used badly, time passes all the same".

The village name commemorates William de Stanford, Lord of the manor in the 13th century, and a later owner, Richard Dyneley, 200 years later.

The meadows are full of wild flowers, and house martins dip down to the water in summer, and that beautiful shrub the guelder rose overhangs the stream at several points. Further along, the field edges are sweet with scented chamomile, growing as a cornfield weed - it looks like a large daisy with feathery leaves. There are poppies and wild pansies, too. In the damp woodlands there are trails of wild honeysuckle and blue flowers of brooklime, a waterside plant, really, that strays into the woods. In the late spring, if you are lucky, you may find the graceful solomon's seal, a member of the lily family, with bunches of small white flowers hanging all the way down its curved stem with the pairs of leaves spread above like wings.

There has been a mill on the little River Pang, which passes through Stanford Dingley since Domesday, and the present building is very attractive, but understandably kept private by its owners.

The river winds off on its way to a rendezvous with the Thames at Pangbourne in one direction, and back across the pastures to its source at Compton in the other. This is one of the most peaceful walks imaginable, broken only by the trickling of the stream over its little weirs. There are several fords and tiny plank bridges with handrails built very much to scale for children on this very clean stream.

Route 4

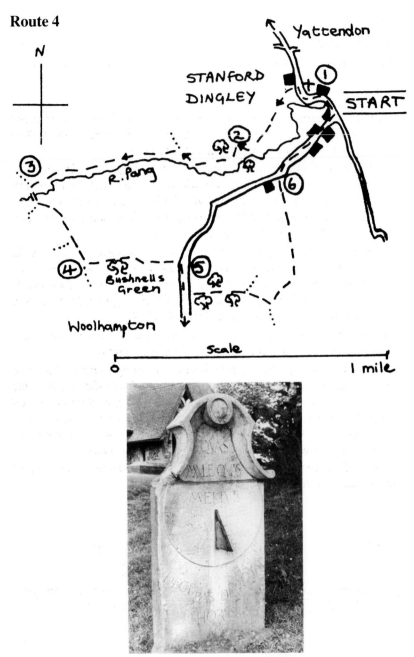

GRAVESTONE AT STANFORD DINGLEY

22

Route 4

Stanford Dingley   3 miles

START   *Stanford Dingley village, (O.S. Sheet 174 SU576715). Park in village.*

ROUTE

1. *From the Bull Inn turn right and follow the road to the church. Turn left on to the marked footpath just before the church, crossing a stile. Follow the trodden path straight across the cattle pasture.*
2. *At the River Pang turn right, climb the gate ahead, and follow the path into the woodland strip. Cross the stile out of the woods and turn left, then follow the riverbank through the fields. At a large shallow ford, with a gate, turn right and follow the open track to a stile. Cross it and turn left. Follow the field path by the river again.*
3. *At the very end of the field cross a stile, continue ahead, then cross the plank bridge (or if children prefer, continue ahead a few yards and wade across the stream at the little ford.) Turn left and follow the field edge to a gate. Go through and follow the path. Go through another gate and follow the path on the right hand side of the field.*
4. *Pass a stile on the right, continue a short distance, then turn left, just before an old gateway, and follow the field edge uphill.*
5. *At the field end cross the stile into the road. Turn right and walk uphill a short distance, then take the marked footpath on the left into the woodland. Follow the track right through the wood. At the end turn left on to the pathway by a fence. Go through the gate at the end and continue ahead into the cattle pasture, keeping the hedge on your left. Go through the gate at the end and follow the hedged lane.*
6. *Turn right at the road and follow it to the T-junction. Turn left and follow the road back into Stanford Dingley.*

Refreshments   The Bull Inn, Stanford Dingley, has outdoor seating and a children's room (lunchtime), and serves food at weekends.

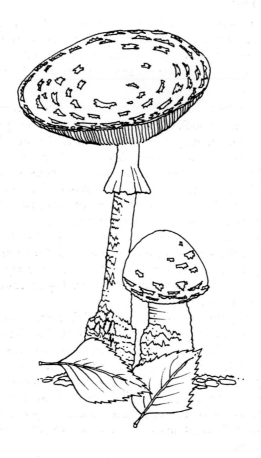

FLY AGARIC Amanita muscaria

Route 5   2½ miles

Ashley Hill

Outline   Warren Row ~ Ashley Hill Forest ~ Dewdrop Inn ~ Pudding Hill ~ Warren Row.

Summary   This short walk takes in the most typical English countryside of deeply shaded lanes, varied woods and lush patchwork fields, up hill and down, open and enclosed by turns. A walk round Ashley Hill is a delight at any time of year and regular visits are ideal for observing the changing seasons.

Attractions   On the south side of Ashley Hill, near Warren Row, is the most perfect sunny woodland of oak and birch with a primeval feel, though it is regularly managed. In the early spring before full leaf shades it in, the leaf litter is full of spring flowers. Fat bunches of primroses, yellow celandines and patches of blue bugle vie for elbow room.

Overhead the chiffchaffs sing their unmistakable song, sometimes losing the second syllable - a sort of chiff with no chaff. They are tiny anonymous green birds, hard to see but easy to hear.

In the clearings, acid-yellow brimstone butterflies flit past, while long-tailed tits collect moss for their complicated bottleshaped nests in the hazel coppices nearby. It really is idyllic. In a wet spring the ground is spongy with water - you can actually hear it trickling under the grass in the glades and open spaces.

On the hilltop the woods are full of wild daffodils, escapees from an old garden, but doing well among the plantations of larch and spruce.

In the autumn the woods are full of curious fungi - it is interesting to see how many different kinds you can find. Look out for fly agaric - striking but poisonous with its cherry coloured cap spotted with white. The spots are the remains of a pale membrane that covers the whole of the young fungus and bursts apart as the cap expands. If you look closely you can see that the stalk stands in a little white cap. The fly agaric grows near pines and birches.

The shady lanes at the hill base are hedged with blackthorn and wild plum, light with blossom in spring, and deeply shaded and secret in the summer.

The small farms set among the folds of Pudding Hill seem straight out of a watercolour, among their green, brown or golden fields, depending on the time of year. Some of them specialise in cattle, and the young heifers will let their curiosity overcome their shyness, come and

continued on page 28

25

Route 5

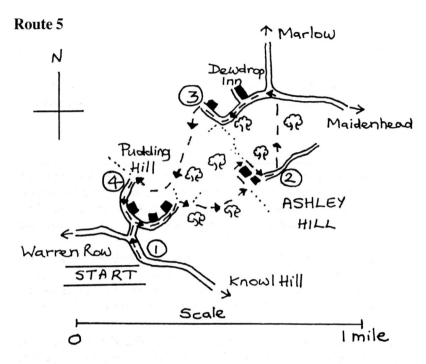

N

↑ Marlow

Dewdrop Inn

③

Maidenhead

Pudding Hill

④

②

ASHLEY HILL

Warren Row

①

START

Knowl Hill

Scale

0   1 mile

WINDSOR CASTLE   Route 7

26

Route 5

Ashley Hill
2½ miles

START *Warren Row 2 miles west of Maidenhead just off the A4 (O.S. Sheet 175 SU817806). Parking places along the minor road south east of the village.*

ROUTE

1. *From the parking place follow the road a short distance then turn right at the next junction. Follow the road round to the right and continue uphill to the end. At the top, take the marked bridleway on the right, continue a short distance, then cross the stile on the right and follow the marked footpath up through the woods.*
   At the hill top turn left on to the footpath and follow it. Turn right immediately after the hilltop house, then turn right on to the track and follow it a short distance. Take the paved road on the left at the top and follow it downhill for about 50 yards, then take the broad woodland track on the left.
2. *Follow this straight down to the bottom of the hill and turn left on to the road. Continue along the road, keeping to the left at the junction, stopping for refreshment if you wish at the Dewdrop Inn, which appears on the right. Leaving the inn, turn right and follow the road to where it ends at a gate. Go through the gate and follow the track through the woods, following the main path round to the right at the crossing of paths, passing a cottage.*
3. *Take the path on the left marked "Footpath to Warren Row", crossing the stile and following the field edge with the fence on the right. Cross the next stile on to the fenced trackway and follow it to the end, passing a stile.*
4. *Cross the stile at the end and turn left on to another trackway. Follow this downhill and round to the left through farm buildings and back to the road. Turn left to return to the starting point.*

have a look at you, and lick your hands with their rough tongues. On this walk they're always on the other side of a fence, so children can approach them with confidence.

Ashley Hill is a place of old lanes that seem to lead nowhere, and houses hidden away. But most of all it is a place for wildlife, and there is always something to see all the year round.

Nearby Attractions The Shire Horse Centre, Maidenhead Thicket, is nearby on the A4.

Refreshments The Dewdrop Inn, Ashley Hill, has a garden and serves food at weekends.

MUSK THISTLE Carduus nutans   Purple   June-Sept.

Winter Hill and Cock Marsh

Outline   Winter Hill ~ Cock Marsh ~ Cookham village ~ Thames bank ~ Winter Hill.

Summary   The Cookham district lies in a loop of the River Thames between the towns of Maidenhead and Marlow. It is an area of sudden contrasts, taking the walker from dry chalk grassland to damp marsh, almost within a single stride, and from flat riverside lands to a high viewpoint, with the Thames-side village of Cookham inbetween.

Attractions   Winter Hill rises up so steeply and suddenly above the Thames that the river is barely visible from the viewpoint at the top, hidden by the little trees of ash, holly and maple that dot the chalk grassland. It is only the cabin tops of passing cruisers that give away its presence. There is a splendid view, though, of the Thames Valley.

In summer the grassy slopes are home to a startling variety of chalk-loving plants, many of them miniature, with blue and purple the predominant colours among the bellflowers and milkworts, with big tufts of droopy-headed musk thistles here and there. There is a strong contrast where chalk meets marsh, and the thickets on the valley floor are often flooded. They, too, have their distinct flowers - especially the unmistakable water violet with its fronds of feathery leaves.

Cookham village is a charming, prosperous-looking place; even the Indian restaurant has Tudor beams! Sir Stanley Spencer, the artist, lived here until his death in 1959. Many of Spencer's paintings covered religious themes but were firmly and reassuringly set in Cookham itself. The most famous is "The Resurrection, Cookham", now in the Tate Gallery, London. The view of the churchyard which appears in the painting can be seen in the course of the walk. There are reminders of Spencer throughout the village - the white-painted house in which he was born, and, nearby, the Spencer Gallery, once the Wesleyan Chapel he attended. The Gallery is open to the public in the summer and is well worth a diversion.

Old Cookham is represented by the Tarrystone, a curious boulder used in medieval times as a meeting point for village sports, and moved to its current position at a road junction in 1909. The Cookham area has a very ancient history of human habitation, as can be seen by the bowl barrows - prehistoric burial mounds that rise clearly out of the cattle pastures of Cock Marsh. It was also one of the first crossing places of the

continued on page 32

Route 6

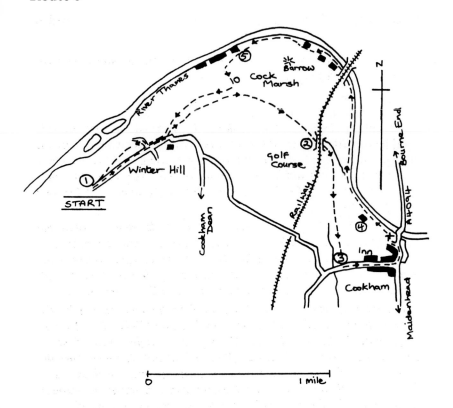

River Thames

Cock Marsh

Barrow

5

10

Golf Course

Winter Hill

START

1

2

Cookham Dean

Railway

Inn

4

3

Cookham

Bourne End

A4094

Maidenhead

N

0   1 mile

Route 6

Winter Hill and Cock Marsh 4 miles

START *At the car park along the crest of Winter Hill about a mile north of Cookham village (O.S. Sheet 175 SU871861).*

ROUTE

1. *From Winter Hill car park follow the road north-east towards Cookham. Continue across the crossroads, and turn on to the track on the left marked Cock Marsh opposite the house called "Chimneys". Follow the track downhill, across a stile, and along the base of the hill. Cross the stile out of Cock Marsh, and follow the same track beside a row of hornbeams.*

2. *Pass under the railway arch, cross the stile on the far side and follow the track again. Take the little flight of steps marked "permitted path" and follow the path with a ditch on the left and Winter Hill golf course on the right. Cross the stile at the end of the track and follow the trodden path across the meadow, emerging in the car park on Cookham Moor.*

3. *Turn left out of the car park and head for Cookham village, passing the Crown Inn on the left. Follow the High Street past Bel and the Dragon Inn, noting the Stanley Spencer Gallery on the right. Turn left at the Tarry Stone into the road signed to Bourne End and Wooburn. Take the track on the left marked "Church" and turn right into the churchyard. Take the gravel path to the left of the church tower, and go out through the gate on to the Thames bank. Turn left and follow the towpath.*

4. *Follow the path past Cookham Reach Sailing Club premises and cross the stile back into Cock Marsh. Keep to the right of the line of pollard willows, and leave the Marsh through the gate marked "the Bounty - Freehouse", passing under the railway bridge. Follow the riverbank past the Moorings Inn, and return to Cock Marsh through the gate. Continue along the bank, noting the ancient burial mound on the left, as far as Ferry Cottage.*

5. *Follow the footpath sign from the Cottage, then turn left on to the marked path, and head back towards the chalk hill. Cross the stile by the pool, and turn right along the valley bottom, and pick up the track back up to Winter Hill, returning by road opposite "Chimneys". At the crossroads, turn right and then take the footpath on the left roughly parallel to the road across the slope of Winter Hill, and return to the car park.*

Thames, with a ferry from earliest times. A passenger ferry still operates from the Moorings Inn.

The Cookham Reach Sailing Club premises stand on the Thames bank just outside the village. At weekends its members take part in sailing dinghy races on the river. These are very competitive and provide great entertainment, especially in windy weather when split-second timing round the race markers causes many a near-collision and brink-of-capsize while avoiding the normal Thames traffic. It is nail-biting stuff to watch!

After the thrills and spills of dinghy-racing, the silent expanse of Cock Marsh, a National Trust property, is another contrast. Its 132 acres are wide open, with Winter Hill standing back in the distance, the damp grassy riverlands populated by lapwing flocks and pied wagtails trotting under the feet of the grazing cattle. There is plenty of room to move out here, even in this crowded corner of Berkshire.

Refreshments A choice of pubs in Cookham village, although the Crown is probably the best bet, with weekend snacks available, and seats outside overlooking play and picnic space on Cookham Moor.

ACCESS BY BUS
Cookham has bus routes to High Wycombe and Maidenhead (The Bee
　　Line).

WINDSOR

Route 7

4½ miles

Windsor & Eton

Outline Eton Wick ~ playing fields ~ Victoria bridge ~ Windsor ~ Eton Wick.

Summary The parkland and playing fields around the towns of Windsor and Eton have a special atmosphere - a curious combination of wild neglect and neat cultivation. This interesting walk takes in the two towns, the winding Thames banks and the open fields and common land.

Attractions The adjoining towns of Windsor and its smaller neighbour Eton are both full of interest and each is famous in its own right. Windsor is a small, prosperous country town of well-to-do Georgian and Victorian houses, presided over by the mighty castle with its impressive walls and great round tower. Even the locals can be forgiven for standing in awe, alongside the American and Japanese tourists, at the foot of this amazing, solid building on its little chalk hill by the Thames. It is the epitome of Englishness.

The town winds itself round the steep side - a tourist haven, where rather posh burger bars rub alongside olde worlde pubs that happily take any currency you can think of, and quite a few you can't. Windsor still manages to retain an air of gentility among the tat, though; a busker plays the lute on the bridge, and stately river launches cruise up and down.

The castle is the largest inhabited castle in the world, and it seems to dwarf the town. It took 900 years to build, overall, with each generation of royalty adding to it.

Eton has the same air of prosperity, and the same air of being dwarfed, this time by the buildings of the college, which was founded in the 15th century, and added to over the years, like the castle.

From the Victoria Bridge (the companion Albert Bridge is farther downstream at Old Windsor), the symbols of both towns can be seen. The castle dominates the view to the left, looming over a loop of the river, guarding the Thames approach to London, while the College chapel, a magnificent building, just rears up straight out of the fields on the right.

There are good clear paths through the famous playing fields and past the boat houses, and there are some exotic residents: the impossibly pretty mandarin ducks, with those orange "sails" on their wings, breed wild on the riverbanks, while the riverside treetops ring to the squawks and chuckles of flocks of wild ringneck parakeets. They are both escapees that have made themselves at home in the Royal park and beyond - but Windsor is an attractive place to foreigners -perhaps it makes them feel at home. *continued on page 36*

Route 7

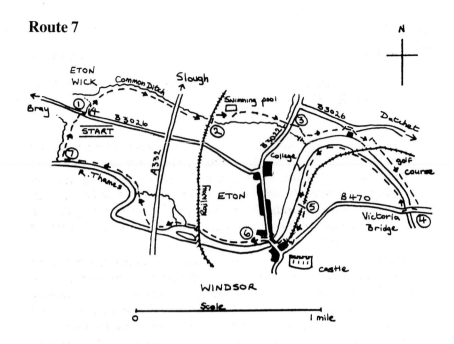

THE THAMES AT WINDSOR

Route 7

Windsor & Eton

4½ miles

START *Eton Wick 1 mile north west of Windsor on B3026 (O.S. Sheet 175 SU947786). Park near the church.*

ROUTE

1. *Take the road west of the church (Sheepcote Road) and follow it round to the right. Ignore a second road joining from the left, and turn right on to the marked footpath. Walk across the meadow, bearing left, and keeping the stream (Common Ditch) on the left. Continue ahead, aiming for the road bridge in the distance. Go through the gate by a footpath marker and under the bridge. Continue ahead, keeping the stream on the left.*

2. *Go under the railway arches, turn left, cross the stream and follow the path by the arches. At the end turn right. Follow the roadway past the golf club, then turn left through a gateway leading to the swimming pool. Turn right at the pool and follow the paved path. Continue ahead through the playing fields, cross the stream and go out on to the road.*

3. *Cross the road and take the marked footpath opposite. Follow it across the cricket fields then turn left on to the marked path immediately before the bridge. At the end cross the stream and turn right on to the road. Follow it a short distance then bear right on to the marked footpath at Boathouse Cottage. Follow the Thames-side path. At the end turn left on to a gravel track, then cross the stile into the pasture on the right, and follow the marked path. Cross a stream, continue into the next field, bearing right, and go through the gate and under the railway arch. Continue on the marked footpath bearing right on to Datchet golf course. Keep to the right hand edge of the course, follow the track to the end and come out through the gate on to the road.*

4. *Turn right and cross the Thames by Victoria Bridge. Turn right on to the riverbank and follow it to the lock cutting. Cross the stile at the end. (Take a detour over the bridge to the left to see the boats in Romney Lock). Go ahead through the boatyard, aiming to the left of the octagonal building, and follow the roadway.*

5. *Cross the railway by the footbridge, and follow the path to the car park. The park here is a good picnic place, and there is a children's play area. Continue ahead to the road and turn right. Follow the road, then turn right into Farm Yard, opposite the Royal Oak Inn. Turn left along the riverbank and recross the river by Windsor Bridge.*

6. *Turn left into Brocas Street, then take the lane by the college boathouse, and come out on to the riverbank. Follow the river bank path, passing a railway bridge and a road bridge. Continue ahead and cross a backwater, ignoring the path on the right immediately after. Continue along the riverbank for about half a mile.*

7. *Take the paved path on the right where a stream flows into the river. Follow it to the end then turn right on to the marked bridleway. Follow it a short way then turn left on to the trodden path across the field, returning to the road at Eton Wick. Turn right and follow the road back to the starting point.*

ACCESS BY BUS

There are bus and train services to Windsor and Eton from Slough and London.

NEARBY ATTRACTIONS Windsor Castle has rooms open to the public.

The Royalty and Empire Exhibition (Madame Tussauds) at Windsor Station.

History on Wheels Motor Museum, Eton Wick.

Refreshments Plenty of choice in Windsor, not necessarily expensive.

RIVER TEST, COMMON MARSH

Stockbridge & Common Marsh

Outline   Stockbridge ~ Common Marsh ~ Test Way ~ Stockbridge.

Summary   Stockbridge lies in the beautiful valley of the River Test. This short walk takes you from the town into the watermeadows of Common Marsh by the river, and back along a section of the Test Way Long Distance Path.

Attractions   Stockbridge, they say, is an unexceptional little town, just a long narrow street. It was a cattle drove town, and cattle are still herded through, mooing unconcernedly and holding up the traffic. But up on the town hall clocktower stands a clue to the place's fame. Yes, even the weathervane is in the shape of a trout, for Stockbridge stands on the River Test, that most delightful and exclusive trout stream.

The town straddles the river which runs beneath the main street in many little strands, so that every other house seems to have a tiny brook rushing beside it. The stream is shallow with a stony bed, but the trout like it, and sometimes there are dozens to be seen. They are remarkably strong fish and can hold a steady position heading into the strongest flow, spotted tails waving gracefully. Quite big trout seem perfectly happy in brooks that hardly seem deep enough to float a tadpole. Late summer is probably the best time to see them.

Common Marsh itself, close by the town, is a little jewel of a National Trust property, an old, grazed watermeadow, with a substantial branch of the Test running down one side. In spring the banks of the river are yellow with marsh marigolds, dotted about with the pale mauve of lady's smocks. In summer it is stunningly pretty -the swift stream fringed with waterplants and crowded with trout. The flowers are all colours - purple loosestrife, blue water speedwell, and the bright yellow of wild musk. There is the trickle of water, the scent of water mint and the blue flash of a passing kingfisher. It is almost the ideal river, springing cleanly out of the chalk hills.

Stockbridge used to stand on the railway between Andover and Romsey - known to its friends as the Sprat and Winkle Line. The line is long ago closed, but the trackway is put to good use along much of its length as the Test Way, a long distance footpath following the river down its valley. The trees alongside have grown tall and the hedges are full of wild hops, forming a lovely green tunnel in places. The trackway itself, though the lines are gone, retains the typical grey pebbles of a railway,

continued on page 40

Route 8

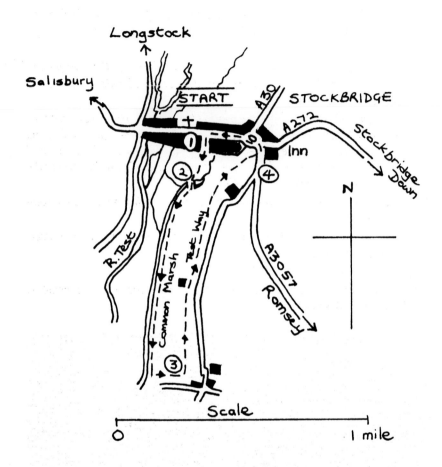

Longstock

Salisbury

START

A30

STOCKBRIDGE

A272

Stockbridge Down

Inn

R. Test

Test Way

Common Marsh

A3057

Romsey

N

Scale

0

1 mile

Route 8

Stockbridge & Common Marsh   2 miles

START   *Stockbridge, on the A30, 5 miles south of Andover. (O.S. Sheet 185 SU358352). There are parking places in the main street.*

ROUTE

1. *Begin at the Wagon and Horses pub in the main street. Take the path to the right of the building, go through the gate, and follow the narrow pathway beside the stream.*

2. *At the end of the path cross the footbridge over the River Test and turn right into Common Marsh. Keeping the river on the right, follow the riverbank as far as the fenced boundary of the marsh. Turn left and follow the fence to the end, then go through the gap in the fence on to the disused railway track (the Test Way).*

3. *Turn left and follow the trackway to the end, coming out on to the road by the White Hart Inn.*

4. *Turn left at the roundabout and go back down Stockbridge main street to the starting point.*

ACCESS BY BUS

There are bus services to Stockbridge from Romsey, Winchester, Andover and Salisbury.

AT STOCKBRIDGE

39

now covered with creeping wild strawberries. Nature soon reclaims the land, but the sites of former level crossings can be identified - the little white pedestrian gates nearby are a giveaway, and it is fun to look for them. There is a certain irony in a railway - the great symbol of progress a century ago - being reinstated as a walkway, and the whole length of it has a haunted feel.

Nearby Attractions   Stockbridge Down, also in the care of the National Trust, is only about one mile east of the town on the A272, and makes a superb picnic place. The high, windy down is in complete contrast to the low meadow of Common Marsh. Skylarks sing constantly over the grass bitten short by hundreds of rabbits, and there are wonderful views from the top, both to the north over the Test Valley, and south to the Isle of Wight, on a clear day. Look out for the juniper trees with their gin scented leaves.

Refreshments   There are plenty in Stockbridge.

FULLING MILL, NEW ALRESFORD   Route 12

40

St. Mary Bourne & the Portway

Outline   St. Mary Bourne ~ the Bourne Rivulet ~ The Portway ~ St. Mary Bourne.

Summary   The village of St. Mary Bourne lies in the gentle valley carved out by its stream, the Bourne Rivulet. The walk takes in the quiet paths behind the village houses, and the hillside beyond, where it crosses the Portway Roman road.

Attractions   St. Mary Bourne is a real picture-postcard village with more than its fair share of lovely thatched houses. There are so many that the chances of finding one in the process of having a new thatch installed are high, and lorry loads of reeds can be met with in the lanes. It is an active community, and you may well find a game of cricket in progress at the recreation ground. There is a children's play area there, too.

The little church - of St. Peter, strangely enough, not St. Mary - is the proud possessor of both a rare black marble font and a "vinegar bible". This is displayed in a glass case, open at the page where the unfortunate printer's mistake, "The Parable of the Vinegar" instead of "The Parable of the Vineyard", is clearly visible. The poor printer has been blamed for this tiny error since 1717.

Outside, under the great yew tree is the oldest tomb in the churchyard, of a father and son of the Longman family who both died young. It has a sad and thoughtful inscription.

The Bourne Rivulet, which gives the village its name flows in and out under the road and among the houses - or sometimes not at all. The flow is unpredictable, and parts of it run dry in summer. Further downstream it is more reliable, and feeds the local watercress beds before joining the River Test at Hurstbourne Priors.

Another unpredictable sight is the Portway, the ancient Roman road that cut through St. Mary Bourne on its way to Silchester (see Route 13) from the west country. The line of it is not easy to pick out, especially when the corn is high - but it is still there, underneath, running straight as a die through this lovely valley with its cornfields and woodland belts. At the southern end of the village, near the Bourne Valley Inn, a house called Portway marks the point where it crosses the main road.

Refreshments   The Bourne Valley Inn has a garden and play area and serves food at weekends.

Route 9

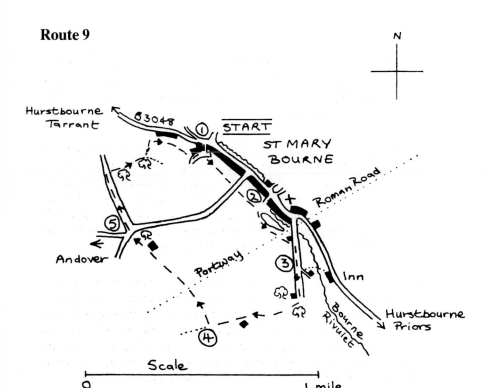

ACCESS BY BUS
Bus service to Andover and Newbury (Hampshire Bus). No Sunday
Service.

Route 9

St. Mary Bourne & the Portway   2¾ miles

START   *St. Mary Bourne village, 3 miles north east of Andover on the B3048 (O.S. Sheet 185 SU423506). Parking is limited in the village, but there are places at the north end near the school.*

ROUTE

1. *Take the small lane beside the school and follow it a short distance to a T junction. Go through the gate ahead marked "T.W.". This is the Test Way long distance path. Bear left across the field to a stile. Beyond it follow the trodden path to the next stile. Cross it and turn left, following the field edge. At the end cross another stile on to the road. Turn right and then immediately left, crossing a stile into a field. Follow the trodden path to the stile at the end. Cross it into the village recreation ground.*

2. *Take a detour here to visit the village church: turn left and go out through the car park into the lane. Follow this down to the village main street and turn right. Cross the road to the church. Retrace your steps to the recreation ground car park. Follow the left hand edge of the ground and cross the stile at the top left hand corner. Follow the marked footpath along the lake edge. At the end turn right on to the lane marked "Test Way", and follow it a short distance until it forks.*

3. *Take another detour here, if you wish, to visit the Bourne Valley Inn. Take the left fork, follow it a short distance then turn left on to the marked footpath over a stile. Follow the trodden path through the field and cross the two footbridges over the Bourne Rivulet into the inn garden. It is well worth the detour just to see the very attractive bourne. You may be lucky, as we were, and spot a water vole among the cresses. Retrace your steps to the fork in the lane and take the other fork this time and follow it uphill. Continue ahead through a small woodland belt, and beyond, until a stony trackway joins from the right.*

4. *Turn on to this track and follow it right across the fields and down through farm buildings to a road junction. Continue straight across the junction and follow the road downhill. At the bottom turn right on to a trackway. Follow this through a woodland belt until it forks. Take the left hand path, cross a stile, and follow the marked footpath along the field edge. At the end turn right and follow along the field bottom to a stile. Cross it and follow the enclosed footpath. Cross the stile at the end and turn left on to the roadway. Follow it a short distance, then turn left again, back to the starting point.*

BERE MILL, WHITCHURCH

Whitchurch & Freefolk ⸙

Outline Whitchurch ~ River Test ~ Freefolk ~ Bere Mill ~ Whitchurch.

Summary Between Whitchurch and Freefolk the infant River Test wanders quietly through the fields. This walk crosses and recrosses the pretty stream giving walkers plenty of opportunity to observe the local wildlife and the appealing scenery.

Attractions The River Test, at Whitchurch, is a wonderful transparent stream, especially near its source, and apart from being very much appreciated by the trout population, it is useful for making very high quality paper - good enough for the bank of England, whose notes were made here until recently.

The area has been famous for its paper mills for nearly 300 years. The current mill is a little way up the valley at Overton, but the first, Bere Mill, was at Freefolk. It was established by Henri de Portal, a French Huguenot refugee, and though the paper making business has moved on, it is still a lovely building, sitting quietly by its rushing stream. The influence of the Portal family may be seen everywhere at Freefolk, from the stunning terrace of thatched cottages they built for their millworkers, to the lichen-covered war memorial, with its pretty streamside garden, dated 1870.

Mills feature strongly in this area, and the showpiece is at Whitchurch. The silk mill is a marvellous building in a lovely setting, perched on Frog Island between two streams of the Test. Only recently it was rescued from ruin - it nearly fell down - and beautifully restored. Silk has been woven here since 1830, and now the looms are working again, some of them powered by the newly operational waterwheel. Very environmentally friendly! The whole mill rattles and rumbles with vibration of the rotating wheel, and the clatter of the winding machines. It's all very hypnotic to watch and not to be missed during a visit to Whitchurch.

Whitchurch is an old coaching town, the meeting point of the London and Newbury roads on the way to Southampton or Exeter. It has just the right dusty look and big houses, and was a market town and borough right back to Saxon times.

Walking in the Test Valley is always a pleasure, with the little river and its side streams slipping in and out of view, bouncing over little weirs

continued on page 48

45

Route 10

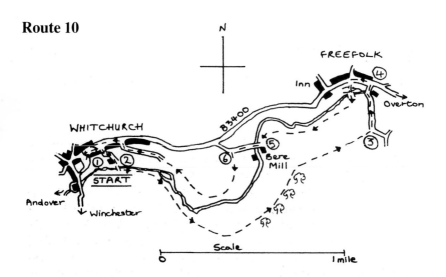

SILK MILL, WHITCHURCH

Route 10

Whitchurch & Freefolk   4 miles

START   *Car parking area in Test Road, Whitchurch (O.S. Sheet 185 SU465482).*

ROUTE

1. *Facing the houses in Test Road, follow the road to the right, crossing the stream. At the T-junction turn right and continue uphill. Turn right into Town Mill Lane, recross the stream, and continue ahead.*

2. *Cross the main stream of the Test at the Town Mill, and take the footpath through the trees on the left. Follow the path, keeping the river on your left. Cross a stile and continue, with a high, chalky bank on the right. Cross another stile and continue into a meadow, with the field edge on the left and a strip of woodland on the right. At the end of the woodland strip bear right across the meadow. Cross the stile in the top right-hand corner, and go through the gateway and follow the righthand edge of the field.*

3. *At the field end go out through the gateway and turn left into the rough lane. Follow the lane downhill, crossing the Test again, and come out on to the main road at Freefolk.*

4. *Turn left and follow the road round past the old war memorial, then take the marked footpath on the left opposite the telephone box. Bear left immediately and cross the side stream by the plank bridge (take care), then follow the trodden path. Cross the second side stream by the footbridge, and continue to the weir. Turn right, cross the main stream of the river, and go through the little gate. Turn right and follow the river. Go through the gateway at the field end, and continue along the right hand side of the next field.*

5. *Cross the double stile at the end and go out through the gate on to the minor road at Bere Mill. Continue ahead, crossing the river again, and follow the road.*

6. *Turn off left at the large gap in the hedge and go into a stony field. Turn left and follow the field edge. The stile is just past the bottom left hand corner. Cross it and follow the left hand edge of the following field. At the far end cross the stile and follow the trodden path on the right. At the end, continue on to the road at Whitchurch. Follow the road round to the right, and turn left at the T-junction. Follow the main road downhill until you reach Test Road. Turn left and return to the starting point.*

and bubbling through pebbly bits. The abundant water means the valley bottom is lush and green, with wild flowers and butterflies everywhere, and thickets of hawthorn and field maple with its helicopter fruits. Sometimes there are nightingales in the thickets. They are secretive birds and like dense cover, but their rich, fruity warbles and throaty chuckles are easy to pick out among the general babble of other birds.

Refreshments The Bell Inn and the Red House in Whitchurch both have gardens, and there is a tea room at the Silk Mill. The Watership Inn at Freefolk.

ACCESS BY BUS & TRAIN
Whitchurch can be reached by bus or train from Andover and Basingstoke.

THE DOWNS AT KINGSCLERE

Kingsclere & the Downs

Outline White Hill ~ Cannon Heath Down ~ Kingsclere ~
Cottington's Hill ~ White Hill.

Summary   A substantial walk among the folds of the north Hampshire
Downs around Kingsclere. The climb up to Cottington's Hill is quite
steep.

Attractions   Kingsclere is racehorse country, and, although you may not
see any unless you visit very early in the morning, evidence of their
presence is all around. High on the downs, the Wayfarers Walk, the long
distance path, passes by the well-maintained exercise gallops, with their
springy, thyme-scented turf. It must be a pleasure to gallop on. There are
hurdles and fences for schooling the horses, and obstacles made of
oildrums and brushwood for their jumping practice.

Cannon Heath Down is a lonely, remote place when the horses
aren't about, and the Wayfarer's Walk wanders on to Watership Down,
which surely needs no introduction. It is a green empty place in these
softly folded green baize hills, and, as the rabbits observed in the famous
book, you can see the whole world from here - well certainly across the
Vale of Clere as far as Newbury - farther on a good day.

The birdsfoot trefoil blooms in yellow cushions in the turf, and it is a
great place for cuckoos in early summer. They make their way along the
hedges at the downs base, calling and squabbling noisily.

Kingsclere itself is a substantial village with some old, pretty houses
and a rather dumpy church set on the green.

Further along the downs is Cottington's Hill, easy to trace by the
huge radio mast at its summit. The downland is wilder here, more
natural, with wild clematis scrambling over the shrubby hawthorns, and
lots of butterflies. The view from the top is worth the steep climb up the
chalky winding paths. Don't miss it.

Refreshments   The Crown, Kingsclere, has a family dining room,
outdoor seating area overlooking the village green, and serves food at
weekends.

Route 11

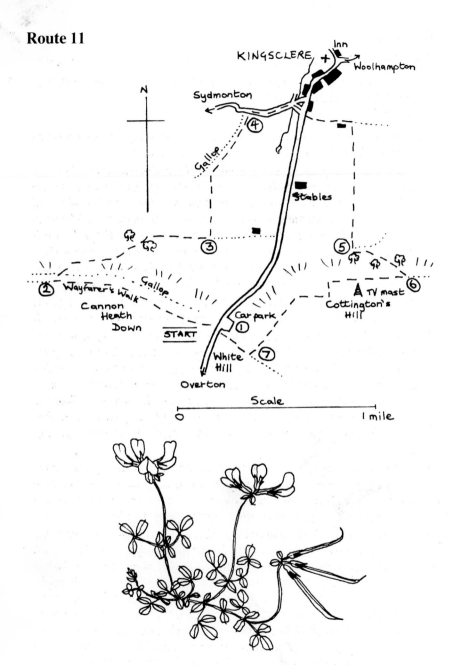

BIRDSFOOT TREFOIL Lotus corniculatus   Yellow/orange   May-Sept.

50

Route 11

Kingsclere & the Downs   5 miles

START   *White Hill car park ¾ mile S.W. of Kingsclere on the B3051. (O.S. Sheet 174 SU517565).*

ROUTE

1. *From White Hill take the Wayfarers Walk heading west and marked "Inkpen Beacon". Follow the walk for about a mile.*

2. *Go through the gate on the right with a yellow arrow marker. Cross the gallop on the trodden path and climb the stile opposite. Turn right and follow the field edge. Cross the stile at the end, then continue ahead to the next stile. Cross the stile then follow the trodden path, as it bears to the left, gently downhill, until a stile in the hedge at the hill base is reached. Cross it and follow the path down through the trees a short way, then turn right on to the chalky track at the bottom. Follow the track to a large gap in the hedge on the left.*

3. *Go through the gap and follow a broad, grassy trackway through the fields until it meets a gallop. Turn right and follow the gallop to the road.*

4. *Turn right on to the road, and turn right again at the next junction into the road marked "Whitchurch and Overton". Cross the stream at the road bridge. If you wish to visit Kingsclere, turn left at the next junction and follow the road to the village centre. If not, turn right at the junction, and then immediately left on to the marked bridleway. When the bridleway meets a paved road, continue ahead past four houses, then climb the stile on the right. Go down on to the gallops, keeping the hedge on the right.*

5. *At the downs base, where the track turns left, take the small path straight ahead into the woods, then turn left on to the woodland track. Follow it a short distance then take the small path on the right - a tree nearby is marked "W.W.". Follow the steep path diagonally uphill.*

6. *At the top, where it meets another track, turn sharp right, and follow the path along the hill top. This downland path is easy to find, but shrubs and undergrowth may obscure it slightly farther along. Keep the hilltop fence on your left all the time. Cross a stile and continue along the hilltop, with the large radio mast close by on the left. Continue until a stile appears on the left. Cross it and go uphill. Cross another stile at the field top and go uphill through the pasture. Cross a third stile at the top, into a narrow pathway and cross another stile out of it. Turn right on to a grassy track and follow it to its end. Cross the stile and turn left into the field. Follow the field edge round to the right, going downhill.*

7. *At the far end cross a stile and turn right on to the Wayfarer's Walk, and follow it back to the car park.*

ACCESS BY BUS

There is a service from Basingstoke and Winchester (Tidworth Silver Star).

NEW ALRESFORD POND

Abbotstone Down & New Alresford

Outline   Abbotstone Down ~ Old Alresford ~ New Alresford ~ River
Alre ~ Wayfarer's Walk ~ Abbotstone ~ Abbotstone Down.

Summary   New Alresford stands near the source of one of Hampshire's
finest chalk streams, the River Itchen, and this substantial walk takes in
the town itself, its damp valley and its wide downland setting.

Attractions   Alresford is a pretty country town, once a coaching stop on
the London-Southampton road, with streets running up and down hill,
full of colourful old houses, most with gateways for the coaches, and
shops full of old curiosities. But its biggest claim to fame is as a producer,
on a grand scale, of watercress. This may seem a lot of fuss about a bit of
garnish - but there is an awful lot of the stuff about. Not only are there the
watercress beds of commercial growers, some of which are visible in the
course of the walk, but it grows wild, too, in every suitable cranny around
the clear chalk streams that bubble along the valley bottom. It is all very
attractive to wildlife, and the enticing piping of wading birds, like the
redshank, can be heard, as well as the non-stop quacking of happy ducks.

   Between the towns of Old and New Alresford stands a large pond.
This was formed when the Alre streams were dammed in the 12th century
by Bishop de Lucy of Winchester to form a reservoir. The main B3046
still runs along the dam top, some feet above the river level.

   The prettiest corner of all is probably the 13th century fulling mill, a
gorgeous black and white building set among the little streams, which
harks back to Alresford's medieval past as a centre for the cloth trade.

   Farther downstream, children will enjoy looking out for a little
gravestone by the path, inscribed: "Here lies Hambone Jr, faithful friend
of the 47th Infantry Regiment, May, 1944". A touching doggy memorial,
I guess.

   Here, too, the watercresses stand aside and the trout take
precedence. In places it seems that water seeps out of the ground
everywhere - and it does. The underlying chalk sends out little springs at
many points, and they run together into tiny brooks before flowing into
the River Alre and at length into the Itchen.

   Even in the lowest, prettiest part of the valley you are never far from
the chalk, which rises up in low hills at the sides. The Wayfarer's Walk is a
long distance footpath that traverses this country close to Alresford. A
broad chalky trackway with impressive trees in its hedges, including some

continued on page 56

53

Route 12

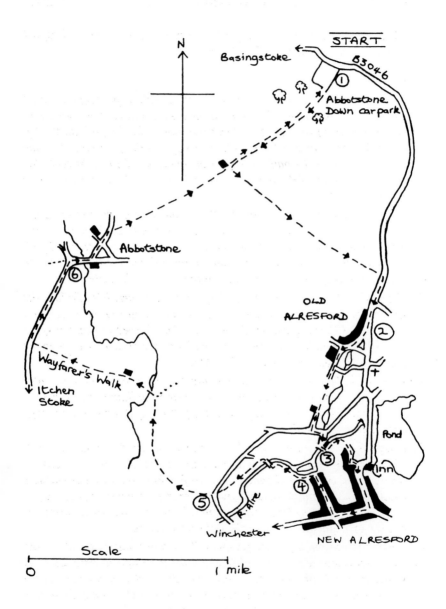

Route 12

Abbotstone Down & New Alresford   7 miles

START   *Abbotstone Down car park, 2½ miles north of New Alresford on the B3046. (O.S. Sheet 185 SU584361).*

ROUTE

1. *From the car park follow the grass track downhill, passing through a gateway into woodland. Continue along the track out of the woods, and at the bottom of the hill, by a farm building, take the path on the left marked "footpath to Alresford". At the top of the field cross the stile and continue on the path until it meets the road. Turn right on to the road and go into Old Alresford (which is actually newer than New Alresford . . .).*

2. *At the village green turn right by the phonebox and then left into the lane. Follow the lane to the end, then take the marked footpath on the left. At the "Private Road" sign, bear right and follow the marked path along the field edge. Cross the stile at the end and continue up to the road. Turn left, then take the small gravel road on the right.*

3. *Cross the River Alre at the fulling mill, and turn left. Follow the streamside path to the T-junction, then turn right into Broad Street, Old Alresford. (The Globe Inn is downhill on the left -see Refreshments). At the top of Broad St., turn right and walk down through the town to the crossroads, then turn right into The Dean.*

4. *At the end of the road, turn left on to the riverbank, and follow the path. Cross the river by a little bridge beside a small building, then cross the side stream. Continue along the path, following it along a field edge until it merges with the road.*

5. *Cross the road and take the trackway marked "right of way" (Wayfarers Walk). Follow it to a junction of tracks. Turn left, cross a stream, and continue ahead. Look out for the trunk of a huge willow with a bunch of mistletoe and small elder tree growing halfway up. At the flint cottage, go straight on uphill. When the trackway meets the road, turn right and go downhill to the next junction.*

6. *Take the road on the right signposted "Alresford and Bighton". Cross the stream and take the small road on the left opposite Mill Cottage. When the road curves left to a farm, take the track straight ahead, then take the marked bridleway on the right. At the farm buildings go straight on and follow the track back to the car park.*

substantial yews, the walk strides out across the empty downland, wandering among the hills. Up in the hills the yellowhammers flit along the hedgetops or sing wheezily of "a little bit of bread and no cheese". (It-it-it-it-it-it-eeze!)

At Abbotstone Down itself there are some wonderful open views across the hills and into the valley of the River Itchen, of which the Alre is a tributary, on its way to Southampton.

Nearby Attraction The Mid-Hants Steam Railway, "the Watercress Line", runs between Alresford and Alton.

Refreshments There are many inns and teashops in New Alresford. The Globe has a garden and play area overlooking the Alresford Pond - a wonderful outlook.

ACCESS BY BUS
There are bus services to Alresford from Guildford and Winchester (Alder Valley).

ROMAN AMPHITHEATRE, SILCHESTER

Silchester & the Devil's Highway

Outline   Silchester Museum ~ Calleva site ~ the Devil's Highway ~ Foudry Brook ~ Silchester.

Summary   The gently rolling plain around Silchester is very much exposed to the wind, and the walls of the Roman city of Calleva are forbidding in winter, so it is best to visit on a fine day. This walk provides an all round view of the city in its open setting, and an opportunity to visit the tiny museum nearby.

Attractions   Walking along the Drove Road, in the middle of what was once the Roman city of Calleva Atrebatum, it is hard to imagine this empty, silent plain as the site of a busy town - only the skylarks disturb it now. But there, all around, is the city wall, overgrown and battered. It is still a complete circuit - octagonal, actually - and a mile and a half all the way round. In between there is open farmland, but underneath the pasture and ploughed fields are the foundations of the most complete Roman town in Britain, complete with forum, temples, and dozens of houses laid out in a grid plan.

Calleva was a regional capital, but, unlike many other Roman towns, no modern town has grown up on its site - and this is why it is so well-preserved. The village of Silchester, which lies outside the walls, is proud of its Roman connections, and there is a tiny museum, open most days, with exhibits explaining the layout and history of Calleva.

One of the few buildings within the walls is the medieval church of St. Mary the Virgin, a pale building, a thousand years younger than Calleva, whose graveyard perches on the very top of the Roman wall by the east gateway. On the western side of the church there is a neat section of a Roman pillar. This once held a bronze sundial inscribed with the cheerful thought "Take heed, Time flies, Rome perished, So wilt thou". The sundial was stolen in the 1950s.

The town wall itself is built of flints set in cement with courses of flat limestone slabs. Trees grow on it and round it, and it is ruined, but it is still magnificent - over twenty feet high in places.

Even more impressive is the newly excavated amphitheatre. This now has a flat sandy floor and a circular flint wall with gates. It looks absolutely ready for action. This amphitheatre would have been a 4,000 seater in its day, and was set outside the walls to prevent 3rd century hooligans from rampaging through the town!

continued on page 60

Route 13

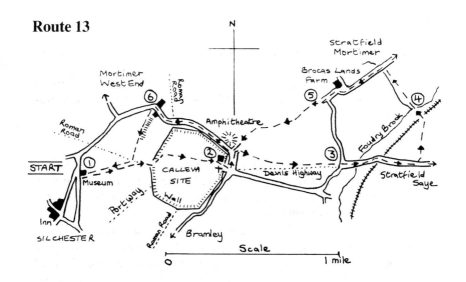

ROMAN WALL, SILCHESTER

Route 13

Silchester & the Devil's Highway   4½ miles

START   *Calleva Museum, Silchester, 1½ miles north east, by minor roads, from the A340 at Tadley (O.S. Sheet 175 SU629624). Park near the museum.*

ROUTE

1. *From Calleva Museum follow the gravel lane. Cross the stile at the end and continue along the track ahead. Go through the gate, then through the wide gap in the Roman walls (the West Gate), and follow the Drove Road across the ancient town.*

2. *Where the track curves left, go through the gate on the right and take the marked footpath towards the church. Go through the small iron gate into the churchyard. Follow the path past the church door and go out through the gate, past the pond and out into the road (Church Lane). Turn left on to the road and follow it past the junction on the right to the marked footpath across the field. Follow the track across the field to the stile. Cross the stile on to the road junction.*

3. *Take the road signposted "Stratfield Saye" and follow it uphill, crossing the railway, and take the marked footpath at the top of the hill on the left. Follow the field edge, keeping the hedge on your left, and then recross the railway by the cattle bridge. Continue downhill with the hedge on the left, then cross the stile.*

4. *Cross the brick bridge across the Foudry Brook, and cross a second stile into the field beyond. This point marks the meeting of two brooks. Follow the track across the field ahead, cross the stile at the end and turn left on to the road. At the next junction take the road marked "Bramley and Stratfield Saye", passing Brocas Lands Farm on the right.*

5. *When the road turns sharp left, follow the hedged track straight ahead until you meet the road again, with the Roman Amphitheatre on the right. Turn right on to the road and follow it for ½ mile passing farm buildings on the right.*

6. *Take the next marked footpath on the left and follow it along the edge of the Roman earthwork. At the end of the path cross a stile ahead into a sheep pasture. Cross the pasture to the stile opposite. Turn right into the lane and follow it back to the starting point.*

ACCESS BY BUS
There is a bus route to Reading (The Bee Line).

Five Roman roads left Calleva, including the great east road to London, later romantically named the Devil's Highway. The church marks its exit point and the walk follows its course, as nearly as possible, for a short distance. You would never guess, to look at this quiet country lane, that it marked the beginning of a great road nearly 2,000 years old.

The Devil's Highway is close to the Foudry Brook, whose feeder streams meet nearby, marking the Berkshire/Hampshire border for a way, and flowing on to join the Kennet and Avon canal at Reading before meeting that other great highway, the River Thames. Just here it is a pretty babbling brook overhung by alders and willows, and trimmed with water dropwort.

All around Calleva there are superb, tall oak trees, still standing despite the gales, and spreading out over the low hedgetops in this open, windy landscape with its quiet ruins.

Refreshments The Calleva Arms, Silchester, has a large garden and play area, and serves food at weekends.

BASINGSTOKE CANAL AT NORTH WARNBOROUGH

Odiham & the Basingstoke Canal

Outline   Odiham ~ North Warnborough ~ Greywell ~ Warnborough Green ~ Odiham.

Summary   This walk includes views of both the old Basingstoke Canal and that charming trout-stream the River Whitewater. Together they occupy the area between the town of Odiham and the village of Greywell - they even cross over at one point. The intriguing route crosses itself twice and can be shortened by omitting the last loop to Greywell.

Attractions   The Basingstoke Canal dates back to 1788, and links Hampshire with the River Wey in Surrey, and thus with the Thames. Until quite recently the canal, superseded by the railways and long out of use, had been allowed to fall into ruin. But now most of the locks and towpaths have been cleared, and leaks in the clay lining repaired, with the aim of bringing it all back into use for pleasure craft. However, the Odiham-Greywell section is still very quiet, and the abundant wildlife remains undisturbed by boat traffic. Swans, mallards, coots and moorhens all breed, and the dabchick, that almost globular waterbird no bigger than a thrush, can regularly be seen feeding its stripey-headed young.

Close by the canal stands the forgotten keep of Odiham Castle, from which King John set out in 1215 to set his seal to Magna Carta at Runnymede. It is the only octagonal keep in the country, but now the ruined walls, eight feet thick are home only to a noisy colony of jackdaws. It is still an amazingly romantic place, hidden away in a little thicket.

Close by the castle the canal crosses a river. The Whitewater is a shallow, babbling stream, full of trout and attended by pairs of grey wagtails. The still waters of the canal pass over it on a low aqueduct, just a foot or two above the fast flowing stream.

At Greywell the canal vanishes into the tunnel which runs under Greywell Hill, and emerges at Up Nately, near Basing, the canal's western end. The tunnel is nearly a mile long, and has been neglected many years. It is closed off by a great grille and is now home to thousands of bats of half a dozen species. It is a strange, rather eerie place, with the gardens of Greywell village ranged along the tunnel top, and the canal itself dead still and clear enough to see the waterplants anchored to the bottom, and small fish swimming among them.

continued on page 64

Route 14

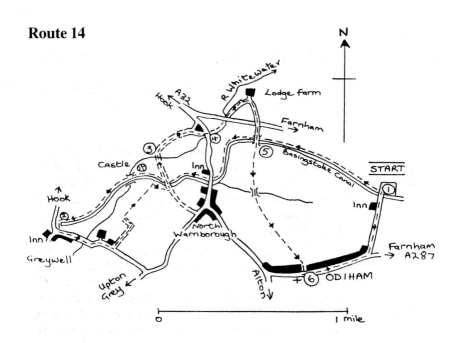

KING JOHN'S CASTLE

62

Route 14

Odiham & the Basingstoke Canal   5½ miles

START   *Odiham Wharf car park (O.S. Sheet 186 SU747517). Take the B3016 from Odiham centre, cross the canal and turn right.*

ROUTE

1. *From the car park go up on to the canal bank and turn right under Colt Hill bridge. Follow the towpath, passing under the bridge by the Swan Inn, North Warnborough, and passing the lifting bridge at Warnborough Green. Continue along the towpath passing King John's Castle and crossing the Whitewater on the little aqueduct. At the Greywell Tunnel, take a diversion down the steps for a closer look.*

2. *Turn left on to the tunnel top and follow the footpath to the road. Turn left and walk downhill, crossing the Whitewater again. Continue past the waterworks to the redbrick house called Skylark Cottage. Turn left on to the marked footpath and follow it round to the stile at the end. Turn right over the stile and follow the path, keeping the hedge on your right. Cross another stile and turn right on to the canal bank. Cross the canal at the lifting bridge, and follow the lane to the ford.*

3. *Cross the Whitewater here on the footbridge or paddle if you wish! Cross the second ford a few yards on, bear right into the lane beyond and bear right again at the house called Applemore, then continue up to the main road, emerging by the mill-pool.*

4. *Cross the road, and take the footpath directly opposite. At the end of the paved track, bear left following the trodden path across the field. Cross the stile and go under the road bridge, crossing the Whitewater once again. Another stile takes you to the paved road leading to Lodge Farm, straight ahead. At the farm bear right, then follow the marked footpath on the right, recrossing the main road on the foot-bridge.*

5. *Cross the Basingstoke Canal again on the open bridge (take care here), and follow the arrowed path along the field edge, with the hedge on the right. Cross the stile in the top righthand corner, then cross the next field to the stile in the middle of the hedge, crossing the stream by the plank bridge. Bear left across the following field to the stile in the top lefthand corner. The last field is crossed to the stile standing on the right of the redbrick house with white windowframes. Follow the passageway and come out in Odiham High Street by the George Hotel.*

6. *Turn left into the High Street, then bear left into the road signed "Basingstoke Canal". Cross the canal and return to the car park.*

Lodge Farm at North Warnborough has an interesting history as the site of two Roman houses, whose foundations were found complete with hypocaust (Roman central heating) and many objects and remains. Now it is a modern farm with a pottery as well as horses, cattle, a fish pond and a flock of black sheep.

Odiham itself is a solid country town of Georgian redbrick, with a wide main street. If time permits, it is worthwhile taking a detour to see the lovely church (the largest in North Hampshire), and the ancient Pest House, where plague victims were cared for.

At Odiham Wharf, if you have any energy left, you can hire a rowing dinghy or take a trip in a longboat - and don't forget to feed the ducks.

Refreshments The Swan at North Warnborough and the Fox and Goose, Greywell both have gardens and serve food at weekends. At Odiham the Water Witch has a play area and gardens running down to the canal.

Nearby Attractions The remains of Basing House, a Royalist stronghold besieged and ruined in the Civil War.

ACCESS BY BUS
There is a bus service to Odiham from Aldershot and Basingstoke (Alder Valley).

THE WAKES, SELBORNE

Route 15

Selborne

Outline   Selborne village ~ the zig-zag ~ Selborne Hanger ~ Selborne village.

Summary   Selborne is a small village with a great deal to offer, so this walk is short to allow plenty of time to explore the other attractions. Nonetheless, the route shows the village from many angles, and gives superb views over the surrounding countryside.

Attractions   Whatever else you may say about Selborne, it is first and foremost the home of Gilbert White, the great 18th century naturalist, who lived most of his life there. His benign presence seems everywhere in this village - and it's enough to bring any self-respecting wildlife enthusiast out in goosebumps.

Above all there is Selborne Hanger, a great dark beechwood, looming up above the village - almost overhead, it seems, on the steep chalky slopes. It has great presence, and you just have to climb it! The way up is the zig-zag, a most impressive pathway - and not nearly as difficult to climb as it looks from the bottom. The views across the valley open out as you go up, and are quite superb from the top, especially in the early spring before the leafy canopy closes in. You can get your breath back by the Wishing Stone at the top. Gilbert White was responsible both for the stone and the zig-zag.

The beechwoods of the Hanger have taken a fair battering from the gales of recent years, and some of the large trees have tipped up -but the light these gaps let into the solid shade has opened the woodland and filled in with wild flowers and the cries of small birds. The steep slopes have an unusual quantity and variety of ferns for this part of the country - especially the hartstongue fern with its long strap-shaped leaves, which forms little forests on the steepest slopes. The wild gooseberry flourishes here, too, as it has since White's time, when he fed them as a treat to his tortoise, Timothy.

The houses of the village appear wavering in and out between the leaves, wherever there is a small gap, with lovely green meadows between them and the chalk hill.

Back in the village, by that postage-stamp of a village green, known as the Plestor, stands St. Mary's church. There was a great drama here recently when the ancient churchyard yew (known to Gilbert White, of course) was blown down in a gale. The village united to try to save it, and

continued on page 68

Route 15

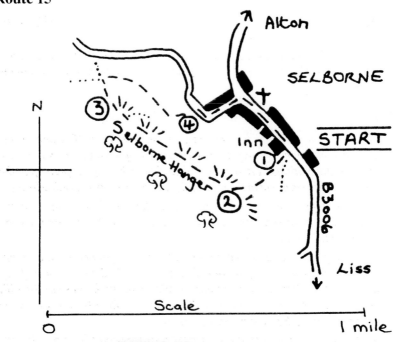

YEW, SELBORNE CHURCH

66

Route 15

Selborne

START *Selborne village 2 miles south of Alton on the B3006 (O.S. Sheet 186 SU743335). Start at public car park beside the Selborne Arms in the main street.*

ROUTE

1. *Take the footpath near the car park entrance marked "footpath to the zig-zag and hanger", and follow it to the base of the hill. Go through the gate into the National Trust property, and take the zig-zag path up to the Hanger. There is a seat at the top for the weary, near the Wishing Stone.*

2. *Take the steps up to the right, and follow the woodland path along the edge of Selborne Hanger. Continue along the path, ignoring a steep path downhill to the right.*

3. *When the path begins to go downhill, at a crossing of paths, take a flight of steps down to the right, and follow the path down, with a sheep pasture on the left. Turn right and continue along the base of the hill, and then cross a stile on the left. Go down the field back towards the village, keeping the field hedge on the right.*

4. *Go out through the gate and turn right into the road (Gracious Street). At the junction with the main street, cross over to the village green, and take a detour round the churchyard. Gilbert White's grave is on the north side of the church. Return to the green and turn left into the main street. Gilbert White's house is just across the road. Follow the main street back to the Selborne Arms, and thus to the car park.*

ACCESS BY BUS
There are bus services to Petersfield and Alton (Alder Valley).

it was set back in the ground - but not before the remains of a dozen or so Saxon burials were found beneath it. Inside the church you can admire the astounding stained glass window installed in 1920 to the memory of Mr. White. This beautiful window shows St. Francis of Assisi with more than 50 species of birds, all readily identifiable and depicted in perfect biological detail and fabulous soft colours. It makes a stunning memorial. The great man's grave, by contrast is a simple stone engraved with his initials.

White's house, The Wakes, stands just across the street and is a charming and sympathetic museum, informally laid out with many of his possessions. Part of the house also commemorates Captain Lawrence Oates, whose family bought the house in the 1950s, and there are interesting exhibits on Scott's Antarctic expeditions. Behind the house is a large garden with a wild air. Old-fashioned bulbs, fritillaries and wild tulips, grow under the trees, and there are curious herbs in the herb garden. And the little rectangular pond contains not goldfish, as you might expect, but a healthy colony of newts - Gilbert White himself could only have approved, as he would of the wild flowers that still grow freely on the banks in this amazingly unspoiled village.

Extra Attraction   the Romany Folklore Museum, Selborne.

Refreshments   The Queen's Hotel and the Selborne Arms both have children's play areas and serve food at weekends. There is also a tea shop in the village.

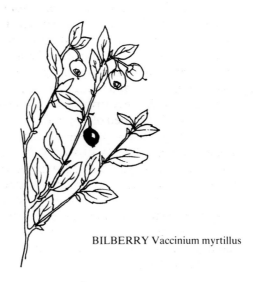

BILBERRY Vaccinium myrtillus

Alice Holt Forest

Outlines Walk one; Alice Holt Visitor Centre ~ Lodge Inclosure ~ Goose Green Inclosure ~ Abbots Wood Inclosure ~ Willow Green Inclosure ~ Visitor Centre.

Walk two; Alice Holt Visitor Centre ~ Glenbervie Inclosure ~ Lodge Pond ~ Visitor Centre.

Summary Two walks in the lovely "Inclosures" or plantation areas of Alice Holt Forest. One is short and easy, using the forest roadways, while the other is longer, more adventurous and takes in the wilder more remote areas of the forest.

Attractions Alice Holt is a forest with a long history, first as a royal hunting preserve in Saxon times, and later as a major source of oak for the ships of the Tudor navy. It is still a 'working forest', under the management of the Forestry Commission, and trees, mainly softwoods these days, are still grown as a crop. However, Alice Holt is far from being one gloomy stand of evergreens. The planting is sympathetic, with plenty of native broad-leaved trees and stands of oak to relieve the monotony of conifer plantations.

The delightful name of the forest dates back to a Saxon Bishop of Winchester, Aelfsige - Aelfsige's Holt, or woodland - which over the centuries became Alice Holt. It was a deer forest in those days, and there are still deer to be seen. They are Roe Deer, small and shy, the bucks with short antlers. There are about 100 of them in the forest, and the slotted prints of their sharp little hooves can often be seen along the edges of the gravel tracks. Their numbers are strictly controlled, as they do great damage in the plantations, and young trees can be seen wearing shields of plastic tubing to keep the deer from nibbling off the bark.

Alice Holt stands on a bed of clay and is criss-crossed with ditches to improve the drainage. Many woodland plants take advantage of these and grow happily along the edges. Among them is the Bilberry, a small shrub of the heather family. It has bright green whippy stems, and small round pinkish-green flowers in spring. In the summer they are followed by delicious purple fruits - tiny but very sweet. Oak and bilberry on a clay soil is a very ancient combination, and is probably a good indication of what the forest looked like in the distant past. Even in dry summers the water-retaining clay keeps the forest looking lush and supports many interesting plants of damp places.

continued on page 73

Route 16

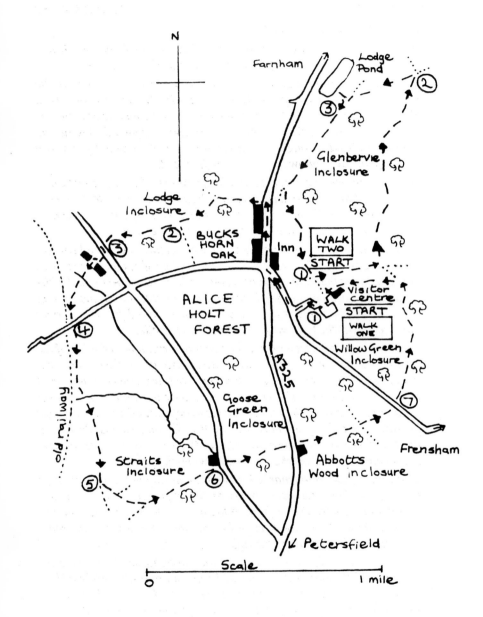

Route 16

Alice Holt Forest

4½ & 2½ miles

ROUTE (Walk 1) Longer walk

START   *Buckshorn Oak, off the A325 Farnham to Petersfield Road. (O.S. Sheet 186 SU813417). Start at the Visitor Centre car park.*

1. *Turn left on to the forest roadway, heading for the main entrance. At the entrance turn right and follow the road to the Halfway House Inn. Turn right on to the main road (use the pavement) and continue past the row of houses. Turn left on to the marked bridleway beyond the last house. Continue ahead through the Forest entrance, then bear left on to a grassy pathway. Follow this path straight ahead.*

2. *At the point where a bridle path joins from the left, keep straight on - fallen trees have obscured the way, but the main track is quite clear a few yards further on. Continue ahead, eventually coming out of the woods. Cross a stile and take the grassy track down to the road.*

3. *Turn left and follow the road a short distance before turning right on to a marked footpath. This track goes round to the right, and then straight ahead between the cottages, skirting one of the gardens. At the end of the garden cross a small plank bridge and a rickety stile. Go straight across the field and cross a stream by a small bridge. Head for the top right hand corner of the following field and cross the stile.*

4. *Cross the road and take the marked footpath running to the left of the disused railway. Follow the railway track through the field, and cross the stream by the plank bridge at the end. Continue along the right hand edge of the following field, crossing a stile and small double bridge over streams at the end. Follow the field edge as before until a prominent post bearing a white footpath marker is reached. Continue across the field in the direction shown on the marker towards the woods. A gap in the trees marks the entrance, reached by a narrow plank bridge.*

5. *Continue ahead on the marked footpath, ignoring paths from the right and left. Follow the path round to the right, emerging at a deer observation tower. Turn left on to the marked footpath, and continue straight ahead. Cross the stile at the end and walk down to the road, using the small gateway on the right.*

6. *Cross the road and take the marked footpath opposite. At the end cross the busy A325, and take the marked footpath opposite. Walk a short distance, cross a stile and continue across a field. Cross another stile and follow the forest track, passing Abbots Wood Nature Trail. At the crossing of the gravel tracks, go straight on. At the hilltop there is a good*

view of the Hampshire Downs. Continue ahead, going out through the gate at the end.

7. *Cross the road into Willows Green enclosure, and follow the marked footpath along a gravelly road. At the junction with a road from the left, keep right. At the next junction, turn left and follow the track back to the Visitor Centre.*

(Walk 2) Short walk

START *For the start to walk two, take the track marked Lodge Pond as far as a grassy pathway, just before the coach park.*

1. *Turn right on to the grassy pathway and continue along the path until it is crossed by a gravel track. Turn left on to the track and follow it straight on, ignoring the second track joining from the left.*

2. *Where the main track forks in two, leave it and take the small path immediately on the left. Follow this path until it rejoins the main track. Turn left on to the main track, and continue ahead. Pass through the gate at the end and turn right, following the roadway into the car park at Lodge Pond.*

3. *Turn right and walk down to the pond. It is quite possible to walk right round this little lake; the path is clear most of the way, but becomes indistinct and overgrown at the south western end - it may be a bit of a scramble to get through. Children will love this - but adults may prefer to omit the circuit of the pond, or walk only part of the way and then retrace your steps. Go back through the pond car park and take the gravel roadway marked 'Visitor Centre and exit'. Follow this roadway back to the Visitor Centre and starting point.*

ACCESS BY BUS
There is a regular service from Aldershot and Haslemere (Alder Valley).

Like many other woodland areas, Alice Holt suffered damage in the high winds of recent years. Much of this has been cleared and replanted, but some exposed areas are left with scarcely a tree standing, and the walk passes through open areas which must have been shaded woodland walks only a year or two ago, but now have clear views to the hills in the distance. They are a sobering reminder of the powers of nature. But, even left alone, the forest will renew itself, and little armies of birch saplings are already pushing up through the debris. Birch is quick to seed and spread, grows fast, and provides shelter for oaks to follow. It is a plant with the true pioneer spirit.

The Lodge Pond is a quiet water, trimmed with willows and luscious waterside plants. There is a picnic place beside it where you can eat to the astounding shrieks of peafowl and other exotic noises from the Bird Garden nearby.

Alice Holt Forest encourages visitors, and their excellent Visitor Centre has information not only on the forest itself, but on all kinds of woodland management and wildlife. It is well worth a visit.

Refreshments   The Halfway House at Bucks Horn Oak has a garden and play area, and serves food at weekends.

Nearby Attractions   Birdworld Bird Garden is nearby - a visit here combined with a forest walk would make a good day out.

KENNET AND AVON CANAL   Route 1

ALICE HOLT FOREST

Appendices

ROUTES INCLUDING STEEP HILLS
Route 15 — *Selborne — 1¾ miles*
Route 11 — *Kingsclere & the Downs — 5 miles*

ROUTES INCLUDING SLIGHT TO MODERATE HILLS
Route 5 — *Ashley Hill — 2 miles*
Route 2 — *Donnington Castle & Snelsmore Common — 2¾ miles*
Route 9 — *St. Mary Bourne & the Portway — 2¾ miles*
Route 4 — *Stanford Dingley — 3 miles*
Route 6 — *Winter Hill & Cock Marsh — 4 miles*
Route 3 — *Aldworth & the Ridge Way Path — 4½ miles*
Route 1 — *Kennet & Avon Canal — 4½ miles*
Route 12 — *Abbotstone Down & New Alresford — 7 miles*

ROUTES ON FLAT GROUND
Route 8 — *Stockbridge & Common Marsh — 2 miles*
Route 16 — *Alice Holt Forest (walk two) — 2½ miles*
Route 10 — *Whitchurch & Freefolk — 4 miles*
Route 16 — *Alice Holt Forest (walk one) — 4½ miles*
Route 13 — *Silchester & the Devil's Highway — 4½ miles*
Route 7 — *Windsor & Eton — 4½ miles*
Route 14 — *Odiham & the Basingstoke Canal — 5½ miles*

WET WEATHER ALTERNATIVES (Completely or partly under cover)
Arborfield Garrison Museum of Royal Electrical & Mechanical Engineers, Arborfield, Berks. Open most weekdays.
Bereford House Museum, Pound Hill, Alresford, Hants. Open all year. Tea Room.
Curtis Museum & Allen Gallery, Alton, Hants. Open all year.
Gilbert White Museum, the Wakes, Selborne, Hants. Open March to October.
Henry Reitlinger Bequest Museum, Oldfield House, Maidenhead, Berks. Open at certain times.
History on Wheels Motor Museum, Eton Wick, Berks. Open at certain times.
Jane Austen Museum, Chawton, Hants. Open all year.
Littlecote House, Hungerford, Berks. Open in summer.
Museum of English Rural Life, Whiteknights Park, Reading, Berks.
Newbury Museum, The Wharf, Newbury, Berks.
Reading Museum, Blagrave Street, Reading, Berks.
Romany Museum, Selborne, Hants. Open Easter-September.
Rotherfield Park, East Tisted, Alton, Hants. Open at certain times.
Stanley Spencer Gallery, Cookham, Berks.

ARTS & CRAFTS CENTRES
Shire Horse Centre, Maidenhead, Berks.
Silk Mill, Whitchurch, Hants. Shop and tearoom.
Viables Centre, Basingstoke. Craft workshops.

HISTORIC BUILDINGS

Alresford House, Alresford, Hants. Open May-September. Tea garden, picnics.
Avington Park, Winchester, Hants. Open at certain times.
Basildon Park, Pangbourne, Berks.
Bohunt Manor, Liphook, Hants.
Cliveden House, Taplow, Bucks.
Great Coxwell Tithe Barn, Berks.
Mapledurham House and Mill, Berks.
Mottisfont Abbey, Hants. Open April-September.
Sandham Memorial Chapel, Burghclere, Hants. Open daily.
South Hill Park, Bracknell, Berks.
Stratfield Saye House, Hants. Open Easter-September. Restaurant, tearoom, picnics.
The Grange, Northington, Alresford, Hants. Open all year.
The Vyne, Sherborne St. John, Hants. Open April-September. Tearoom, giftshop.
Windsor Castle, Berks (St. Georges Chapel, State Apartments, the Round Tower).

OTHER PLACES OF INTEREST

BUILDINGS

Basing House (ruins), Basing, Hants. Open April-September. Tearoom.
Donnington Castle (ruins), Newbury, Berks. Open all year.
Calleva Roman ruins, Silchester, Hants. Open all year.

WILDLIFE

Birdworld, Holt Pound, Farnham, Surrey. Open all year.
Child Beale Wildlife Trust, Pangbourne, Berks. Special area for children. Woodland Trail, Billbrook, Bracknell, Berks.

COUNTRY PARKS, VIEWPOINTS

Caesar's Camp, Nine Mile Ride, Finchampstead, Berks. Public recreation area.
California Country Park, Finchampstead, Berks.
Danebury Ring, Stockbridge. Heritage site, public amenity area.
Dinton Pasture Country Park, Woodley.
Finkley Down Museum & Country Park, Andover, Hants. Open April-Sept. Shop, Cafe, picnics.
Selborne Hill (viewpoint).
Simons Wood, Finchampstead.
Wellington Country Park, Hants. Museum, lake.
Windsor Great Park, Windsor, Berks. **Windsor Safari Park and Sea World,** Berks.
Yateley Country Park.

SPORTS & LEISURE CENTRES

Alton Sports Centre, Chawton Park Rd., Alton, Hants.
Bracknell Spots & Leisure Centre, Bagshot Road, Bracknell, Berks.
Coral Reef Waterworld, Nine Mile Ride, Bracknell, Berks.
Cotswold Sports Centre, Downs Way, Tilehurst, Reading, Berks.
Downland Sports & Recreation Centre, Compton, Berks.
Edgbarrow Sports Centre, Grant Road, Crowthorne, Berks.
Kennet Sports Centre, Stoney Lane, Thatcham, Newbury, Berks.
South Reading Leisure Centre, Northumberland Avenue, Reading, Berks.
Windsor Leisure Pool, Clewer Mead, Stovell Road, Windsor, Berks.

RAILWAY

Watercress Line Railway, Alresford, Hants. Open March-October.

FOR BUS TIMETABLES

Alder Valley. Tel. Aldershot 23322.**Hampshire Bus.** Tel. Winchester 52352.
The Bee Line. Tel. Reading 581358.

BOAT SERVICE

Salter's Passenger Boat Services (Thames). Tel. Windsor 865832.

DONNINGTON CASTLE   Route 2

FAMILY WALKS SERIES

Family Walks in the Lake District. Barry McKay. ISBN 0 907758 40 1.

Family Walks in West Yorkshire. Howard Beck. ISBN 0 907758 43 6.

Family Walks in Three Peaks and Malham. Howard Beck. ISBN 0 907758 42 8.

Family Walks in South Yorkshire. Norman Taylor. ISBN 0 907758 25 8.

Family Walks in Cheshire. Chris Buckland. ISBN 0 907758 29 0.

Family Walks in the Staffordshire Peak and Potters. Les Lumsdon. ISBN 0 907758 34 7.

Family Walks in the White Peak. Norman Taylor. ISBN 0 907758 09 6.

Family Walks in the Dark Peak. Norman Taylor. ISBN 0 907758 16 9.

Family Walks in Snowdonia. Laurence Main. ISBN 0 907758 32 0.

Family Walks in Mid Wales. Laurence Main. ISBN 0 907758 27 4.

Family Walks in South Shropshire. Marian Newton. ISBN 0 907758 30 4.

Family Walks in the Teme Valley. Camilla Harrison. ISBN 0 907758 45 2.

Family Walks in Hereford and Worcester. Gordon Ottewell. ISBN 0 907758 20 7.

Family Walks in the Wye Valley. Heather and Jon Hurley. ISBN 0 907758 26 6.

Family Walks in the Cotswolds. Gordon Ottewell. ISBN 0 907758 15 0.

Family Walks in South Gloucestershire. Gordon Ottewell. ISBN 0 907758 33 9.

Family Walks in Oxfordshire. Laurence Main. ISBN 0 907758 38 X.

Family Walks around Bristol, Bath and the Mendips. Nigel Vile. ISBN 0 907758 19 3.

Family Walks in Wiltshire. Nigel Vile. ISBN 0 907758 21 5.

Family Walks in Berkshire and North Hampshire. Kathy Sharp. ISBN 0 907758 37 1.

Family Walks on Exmoor and the Quantocks John Caswell. ISBN 0 907758 46 0.

Family Walks in Mendip, Avalon and Sedgemoor. Nigel Vile. ISBN 0 907758 41 X.

Family Walks in North West Kent. Clive Cutter. ISBN 0 907758 36 3.

Ready Spring 1992

Family Walks in the Weald of Kent and Sussex
Family Walks in North Yorkshire
Family Walks around Luton and Dunstable
Family Walks in Northumbria
Family Walks in Nottinghamshire
Family Walks on the Isle of Wight
Family Walks in Clwyd
Family Walks in Dorset
Family Walks in Rossendale, Pendle and Bowland

Other titles under consideration

The Publishers, D. J. Mitchell and E. G. Power welcome suggestions for further titles in this Series; and will be pleased to consider other manuscripts of Derbyshire and regional interest from new or established authors.
